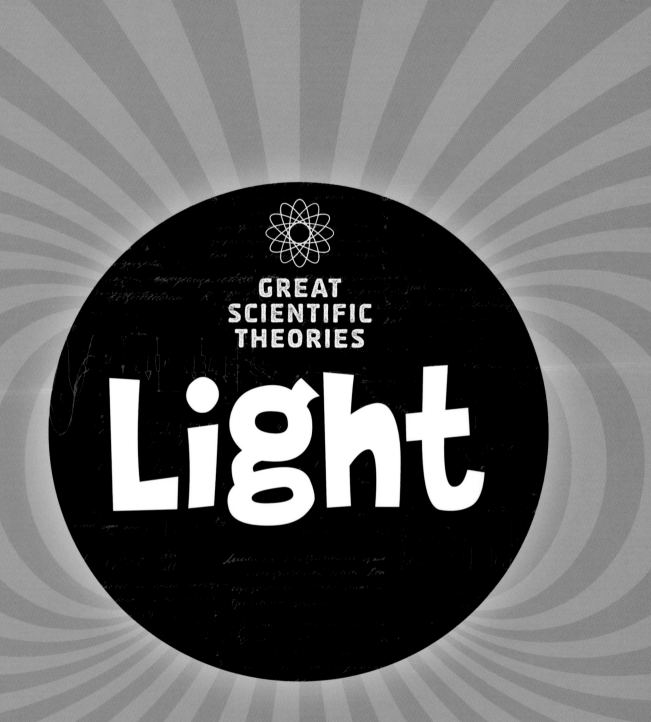

GREAT SCIENTIFIC THEORIES

Light

Richard and Louise Spilsbury

capstone

Published by Raintree, a Capstone Imprint
1710 Roe Crest Drive, North Mankato, Minnesota 56003.
www.mycapstone.com

Library of Congress Cataloging-in-Publication Data
Library of Congress Cataloging-in-Publication data is available on the Library of Congress website.

ISBN 978-1-4109-8728-0 (library binding) — ISBN 978-1-4109-8732-7 (paperback) —
ISBN 978-1-4109-8736-5 (eBook PDF)

Summary:
This book looks at the historical controversies that surround the discovery and theories of light and tells the stories of the scientists who worked on them. It also examines how the different theories based on light were arrived at, how they were tested, and what impact these theories and discoveries have had on our understanding of science today.

This book has been officially leveled by using the F&P Text Level Gradient™ System.

Editorial Credits
Helen Cox Cannons, editor; Terri Poburka, designer; Morgan Walters and Tracey Engel, media researchers; Steve Walker, production specialist
We would like to thank Dr. Rohini Giles at NASA's Jet Propulsion Laboratory for her invaluable help in the preparation of this book.

Photo Credits
We would like to thank the following for permission to reproduce photographs: Alamy Stock Photo: Ian Dagnall, 18, Mary Evans Picture Library, 7, Photo Researchers, Inc., 9, Roger Bamber, 8, sciencephotos, 17; Getty Images: Apic, 14, Central Press, 19; Newscom: akg-images, 16, Album/Documenta, 11, Oxford Science Archive Heritage Images, 13, Pictures From History, 12; Shutterstock: antoniodiaz, 10, asharkyu, 25, Beloborod, 24, Everett Historical, 21, Golden Shrimp, cover, design element (mathematical background), irin-k, 5, Lucy Menshov, 4, Maria Dryfhout, 27, mirtmirt, 6, Nattle, 28 (top), Nicku, 28 (middle left), Olexandr Taranukhin, cover, Preto Perola, 15, saki80, 28 (bottom), Scanrail1, 23, VICHAILAO, 20, Vladimir Nenezic, 26, Wayne0216, 22.

TABLE OF CONTENTS

Some words are shown in bold, **like this**.
You can find out what they mean by
looking in the glossary.

TESTING THEORIES

For hundreds of years, scientists have tried to explain things by coming up with ideas about the way things work. These scientific ideas are known as hypotheses. When scientists believe they have enough **evidence** to show their idea is correct, the idea becomes a **theory**.

Right or Wrong?

Scientists test ideas to see if they are right or wrong. They put together facts produced by these tests to help prove their ideas. Scientists test new ideas all the time, but their ideas are built on the theories of scientists who came before them. Some of history's greatest scientists completely changed the way people thought about the world.

The invention of the sundial shows that people used the position of shadows to find the time of day. The first one was invented by the Egyptians in around 800 BC.

Crops, such as corn, use sunlight to turn air and water into food. They use the food to grow and develop.

Studying Light

Imagine a world without light. Light is vital for most living things: plants use light to make food, and animals need light to hunt or to see approaching dangers. We need light to read, work, travel, and play. People have always known that light and dark have a huge impact on our lives. However, it took many years to discover where light came from, what it is, and how it behaves. Many thinkers and scientists have studied light throughout history.

THE NATURE OF LIGHT

Today, it is common knowledge that light is a kind of energy, such as heat and electricity. Energy is the ability to do work. But our understanding of the nature of light energy has changed greatly through history.

Light from Eyes

The ancient Greeks believed everything was made up of different mixes of four elements: earth, air, fire, and water. Empedocles (495–430 BC) had a theory about how people see that was based on the four elements. He said that the goddess Aphrodite lit fire in human eyes. People saw when this fire, or light, shone from their eyes. There was a problem with this theory, though. People could not see things well at night. Empedocles and his followers said this happened because fire from the eyes was canceled out by different fire from other objects.

Ancient Greek thinkers believed that eyes produce light to see things.

Light Ideas

Empedocles had other ideas about light. For example, he believed light travels with a fixed speed and in straight lines. Scientists today agree with this idea. However, Empedocles also believed that humans see different colors due to an **imbalance** of the elements. Today's scientists wouldn't agree with this theory!

OBSERVING NATURE

The Greeks learned a lot about light from **observing** nature. For example, one reason they thought light came from the eyes was because cats' eyes shine at night. We now know this is caused by light reflecting from inside their eyes.

Empedocles

Light from the Sun

Not all ancient thinkers agreed with Empedocles. In 55 BC, Lucretius (99–55 BC) had an idea that sunlight is pushed out from the sun. No proof of this theory was found until about 1,000 years later.

Dark Room

The Iraqi scientist Al-Hasan Ibn al-Haytham (AD 965–1039) agreed with Lucretius' idea. He also said that we see because light enters our eyes from light sources, such as the sun or anything that light reflects from. He proved this by inventing the camera obscura.

People marvel at the images in a camera obscura today, just as they did in al-Haytham's time.

Camera obscura means dark chamber, or room. The room had a pinhole in a window shutter. Al-Haytham demonstrated how an eclipse of the sun could be seen on the wall inside, opposite the hole. As the eclipse was happening outside, he proved light from the sun had come inside through the hole and into the darkened room.

Reversed Image

The image was reversed. Al-Haytham realized that light rays from the image crossed as they passed through the hole. The image was bigger if the wall was further from the hole. This is because longer distances allow rays to widen before hitting the wall.

BIOGRAPHY

AL-HASAN IBN AL-HAYTHAM

Al-Hasan Ibn al-Haytham was from an area now known as Iraq. After getting in trouble with an Egyptian ruler he was working for, al-Haytham pretended to be crazy so that he was locked in his house instead of being killed. During this time, al-Haytham studied and wrote books about how we see and about light, rainbows, stars, and eclipses.

BENDING LIGHT

Since ancient times, people have wanted to see small things and distant things better than they can with their own eyes. People now know that lenses can do the job by bending light.

Refraction

Refraction is the way light changes direction when it moves from air into **denser** substances like water and glass. In ancient Rome, the **astronomer** Ptolemy (AD 100–168) was the first to record how sticks looked bent in water. He realized this had something to do with how light moved through water. The Romans tested refraction in different shapes of glass. Pieces of glass that were thicker in the middle than the edges made objects appear bigger. This shape of glass was given the name *lens* from the popular Roman food of the same shape: the lentil!

Lenses in eyeglasses were an invention that used refraction. Billions of people around the world use eyeglasses to see better.

Roger Bacon

Seeing Better with Lenses

In the Middle Ages, the English monk Roger Bacon (1214–1292) studied light and vision. He read al-Haytham's books. Bacon realized that lenses work by bending, or **focusing**, light from objects onto the back of the eye. He had a theory that some people cannot see things either up-close or far away clearly because their lenses do not focus light properly. Bacon reasoned that different lens shapes could adjust this focus to correct farsightedness and nearsightedness.

THE FIRST EYEGLASSES

The first eyeglasses in the world were invented in Pisa, Italy, in 1268. The lenses were probably glass discs cut from a glass **sphere**. They were mounted in a wooden frame held to the eyes by handles.

Magnifying with Glass

Have you ever looked at objects with a magnifying glass? A magnifying glass refracts light through a **convex** lens. This tricks our eyes into seeing small things bigger than they really are.

Planet Gazing

By the 1600s, people began to experiment with lenses to help them see distant objects better. In 1608, a Dutch eyeglasses maker, Hans Lippershey (1570–1619), invented the first telescope. It had a **concave** lens eyepiece on a tube with a convex lens inside. Lippershey called his invention a *kijker*, which means "looker" in Dutch.

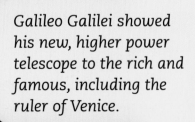

Galileo Galilei showed his new, higher power telescope to the rich and famous, including the ruler of Venice.

CHILD'S PLAY

Two children were playing with lenses in Lippershey's shop. They held up two lenses and looked through them both, focusing on a church nearby. The children showed Lippershey how the church looked bigger and clearer through the lenses. Lippershey based his telescope design on their discovery.

Better Telescopes

From 1609, Italian scientist Galileo Galilei (1564–1642) improved Lippershey's design. He knew the convex lens would bend light from a distant object inside the tube. He reasoned that the concave lens would magnify the image if it was positioned where the image was focused. Galileo experimented with the exact sizes, shapes, and positions of lenses to make his telescope better. Then he did something new. He looked at the night sky through his telescope and saw things people hadn't seen before. For example, the moon had a rough surface, not a smooth one, and other planets like Jupiter had moons. Since then, telescopes have made it possible to see much more of the universe.

INSIDE LIGHT

Light from the sun appears white. In the 1600s, people understood that we see things because sunlight reflects off them, but not why things have different colors. They could not explain how rainbows form. That all changed with Isaac Newton (1643–1727) and his study of **prisms**.

Prism Power

A prism is a triangular piece of glass. It was well known that shining white light at a prism made it produce bands of colored light. In those days, people thought white light was a pure form of energy. They believed it was made impure by moving it through glass. The impure light had different colors.

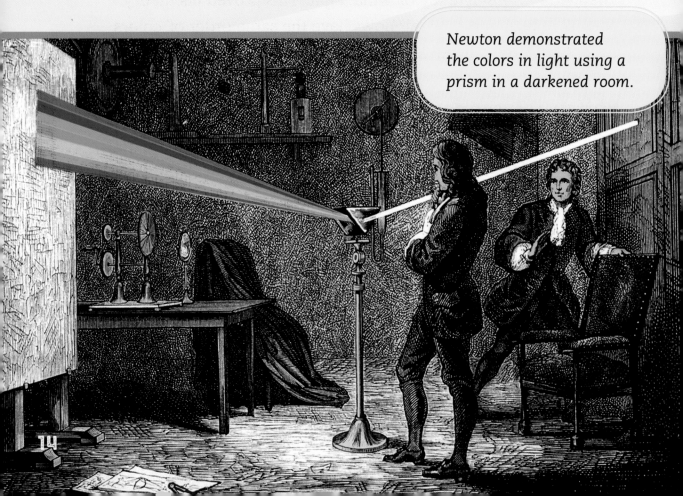

Newton demonstrated the colors in light using a prism in a darkened room.

ISAAC NEWTON

It is said that Isaac Newton described the force of **gravity** after observing apples fall straight to the ground from trees. However, this is not actually true. Newton created laws of motion still used today that are based on forces acting on objects. As well as giving us a better understanding of light, he worked in **astronomy**, math, and chemistry.

Colors of Light

Newton had a theory that the colors are hidden within white light. He tested this in 1666 by placing a second, upside-down prism in the path of the colored light. The different colored rays changed into a single ray of white light. This proved his theory. Newton **observed** how rainbows have the same order of colors as a prism. He realized that rain refracts white sunlight into different colors.

When a beam of sunlight shines down, it is usually white. But, if the light beam hits raindrops on the way down, the raindrops can separate the light into different colors.

What is Light?

In Newton's day, most people thought light was made up of extremely tiny pieces called **particles**. Newton thought each color of light had particles of a different weight. Glass particles in the prism **attracted** these particles by different amounts. That explained the different bands of colored light.

New Wave

In 1690, Christiaan Huygens (1629–1695) published a new theory about the nature of light. He believed that light is made up of tiny waves. Waves are up and down movements of energy traveling in one direction. This theory could not be proven, though.

Christiaan Huygens

Thomas Young

Then, in 1801, the English scientist Thomas Young (1773–1829) shone light on a barrier with two very small slits in it. This created a pattern of bright and dark bands on a wall on the other side of the barrier. There were light bands where the tips of waves met. There were dark bands where the tips met the lowest parts of the wave to cancel each other out. Young realized that if light was made up of particles, there would be only two thin lines of light. The wave theory was correct.

WAVE OF PARTICLES

Thomas Young's experiment showed that light behaved like a wave. But a century later, in 1905, Albert Einstein (1879–1955) conducted his own experiment which showed that light behaves like a particle instead. These particles of light were later called **photons**. Einstein said that electricity moves through certain materials when light shines on them because photons crash into them. Today, scientists agree that light behaves like both a wave and a particle. So Newton and Huygens were both partly right!

LIGHTING UP THE WORLD

Throughout history, people have created their own sources of light, from candles to gas lamps. The main source of artificial light today is electricity.

Bright Spark

In 1802, British scientist Humphry Davy (1778–1829) was the first person to demonstrate a continuous light using electricity. Electricity is the flow of incredibly small particles called **electrons**. Davy had a theory that electrical flow could produce a bright spark. He proved this by showing off a new invention to an audience of scientists.

Across a Gap

His machine had two carbon rods hooked up to a battery. A battery is a device containing chemicals that produce electricity.

Humphry Davy

When he moved the rods together, bright sparks leapt between them. The sparks flew when electrons in one rod moved to the other. This light was bright because the electricity made carbon **vapor** glow. This gas was produced when the rod tips got white hot after electrons built up and heated the carbon. The arch shape of the spark gave this invention its name: the arc lamp.

ARC LAMPS

Early arc lamps did not work well. Sparks could escape and start fires. The spark gap got too big as carbon in the rods burned away. But by the late 1800s, scientists had designed arc lamps with tougher rods. They were enclosed in glass to contain any sparks. These were used as street lamps because they were cheaper and brighter than gas street lighting. The light was too powerful for use inside homes, but was perfect for lighting up stadiums and searchlights.

Arc lamp searchlights were used to light up the sky to help spot enemy planes in World War II.

Universal Light

In the early 1800s, there was greater demand for electric lighting. Electric lights were needed, not only to light up streets and homes but also for the increasing numbers of factories making goods. The race was on to make long-lasting light bulbs.

Glowing Threads

Some scientists thought that **incandescent** materials could be used to create electric light. Incandescent means something that glows when it gets hot. Humphry Davy observed platinum metal strips glowing white when electricity flowed through them. This happened because the thin metal was a resistor. Resistors slow down the flow of electric current. When the electrical energy was slowed, some of it changed into heat and light energy.

Filaments

Later, scientists developed thinner wires with greater resistance called filaments. The filaments glowed better than the wider strips but did not last long because they burned away in the heat. Scientists thought that the filaments would last longer in a **vacuum**, which is a space without air.

Filaments in older bulbs glowed but also heated to burning temperatures when they were switched on.

That's because most materials need air to burn. With no air, filaments could not burn, so they would remain incandescent for longer. However, scientists would only prove this theory later in the 1800s when better vacuum pumps had been invented.

Breakthrough Moment

LIGHT BULB MOMENT!

Around 1879, U.S. inventor Thomas Edison (1847–1931) created a light bulb with a carbon filament made from sewing thread. This glowed in a vacuum bulb. It was a great invention but not entirely his own. Five years earlier, Canadian Henry Woodward invented a nearly identical bulb but had no money to make more. Edison bought the idea and improved the design with better filaments.

Thomas Edison and his team tested thousands of designs for light bulbs.

Light with Less Energy

In the late 1800s, scientists knew that incandescent bulbs turned only five percent of the energy into light. The rest was wasted as heat. So the search began for more energy-efficient electrical lights.

Lower Energy Bulbs

In 1901, U.S. inventor Peter Cooper-Hewitt (1861–1921) invented the mercury vapor lamp. Electric current heated mercury metal inside a sealed tube. It turned into vapor that glowed bluish-green. Scientists working for Thomas Edison painted the inside of such tubes with phosphor. Phosphor is **fluorescent**, which means it glows after it absorbs energy. Their fluorescent lights worked but could not be made cheaply enough until 1934.

Tube to Bulb

Fluorescent tubes use 75 percent less power than incandescent bulbs and last longer. But the tubes did not fit into many common household light fittings. In the 1970s, there was an energy crisis in the United States, so people had to use less power. In 1976, U.S. scientist Ed Hammer (1931–2012) coiled a narrow tube into a compact fluorescent lamp. People thought the coiling would reduce the amount of light the lamp produced. Hammer proved them wrong.

Electronic Light

The most recent artificial lights are light emitting diodes (LEDs). LEDs use a thousandth of the power of an incandescent bulb. In 1961, U.S. scientists James Biard (born 1931) and Gary Pittman (1930–2013) were studying some special materials called **semiconductors** when they saw them glow. This happens after electrons passed through them in one direction. LEDs are tiny but can be grouped to make stronger lights.

Many TVs and computer monitors have screens with lots of LEDs inside to light up the images.

LIGHT DIRECTIONS

During the 1900s and 2000s, scientists have found new ways to use light. This has helped to change our world.

Light Fibers

In 1870, Irish scientist John Tyndall (1820–1893) shone light into a jug of water and poured lit-up water into a bowl. Tyndall had demonstrated internal reflection, where light reflects inwards from the edges of a material. In the 1950s, scientists developed glass fibers that use internal reflection. The first use of these fibers was in an **endoscope** that doctors could use to see inside a patient's stomach. This helped them to see why the patient was ill.

Endoscopes use internal reflection. They are still important tools for surgeons today.

Signals of Light

In the 1960s, U.S. scientist Charles Kao (born 1933) had a remarkable new theory. He believed that information could be sent faster and farther as patterns of light flashed through fibers rather than as signals of electricity through normal wires. People said it was impossible because endoscopes could not carry light very far. Kao said the glass needed to be pure. By the early 1970s, companies had developed pure glass **fiber optic** cables and proven Kao correct.

What Fiber Optics Do

Fiber optics carry extraordinary amounts of information very fast. For example, they can carry 400 DVDs' worth of data over 4,350 miles (7,000 kilometers) in one second. With fiber optics, we can stream videos, watch cable TV, and connect with people worldwide using social media and cell phones. Fiber optic cables cross ocean floors, linking the whole world.

Fiber optic cables can contain hundreds of individual fibers, each barely thicker than a human hair.

Strengthening Light

In 1917, Albert Einstein had another theory about photons. He thought some substances struck with photons would produce more photons. This meant that light could make the substances produce stronger light. Einstein thought making light more powerful could make it a useful energy source.

Inventing the Laser

In 1960, U.S. scientist Theodore Maiman (1927–2007) proved this theory when he invented the first laser. Maiman's laser had a powerful fluorescent lamp coiled around a cylinder of ruby crystal in a darkened tube. When the lamp flashed, its photons caused the ruby to make more photons. The light reflected back and forth between mirrors at each end of the tube. This sped up the photons. Eventually photons burst through one mirror in a powerful, narrow, and controlled beam of light. Light from other light sources spreads out. This laser beam was the same width along its length.

Lasers control and direct powerful light for different jobs, such as slicing through materials.

Lasers inside drones help to measure the angles that the drones turn or dive.

LIGHT LENGTH

Lasers can measure distances accurately. The first men on the moon left a mirror there so scientists could flash lasers toward it to measure the moon's distance from Earth. Amazingly, they have found it is getting further from Earth each year!

Lasers Today

Laser beams can be focused with pinpoint accuracy. High-powered lasers can be used as a precision cutting tool. They can be used in eye surgery or for cutting thick steel in factories. Lower power beams can change the tiny bumps on a CD surface into music or measure the lines in bar codes that identify a product bought in the shops.

QUIZ

1. Where did the ancient Greek thinker Empedocles believe light came from?

2. Who invented and demonstrated the first camera obscura?

3. What is the word used to describe how light bends or changes direction in different materials?

4. Does light move faster in air or water?

5. The lens gets its name from what type of food?

6. Hans Lippershey invented a device for seeing distant objects using lenses in 1608. What is it called?

7. Which device did Isaac Newton use to demonstrate that white light contains different colors?

8. Are particles of light called photons or electrons?

9. Henry Woodward invented this device, but Thomas Edison made a much more famous version of it. What is it?

10. Which device uses intense light to cut and read information?

For the answers to this quiz,
see page 31

TIMELINE

495–430 BC Empedocles says that people see when fire shines from their eyes

55 BC Lucretius suggests that sunlight is pushed out from the sun

AD 100–168 Ptolemy realizes light moves differently through water than it does through air — it refracts

AD 965–1039 Al-Haytham suggests people can see because light enters our eyes from light sources; he invents the camera obscura

1214–1292 Roger Bacon reasons that different lens shapes could correct farsightedness and nearsightedness

1268 The first eyeglasses are invented in Pisa, Italy

1608 Hans Lippershey invents the first telescope

1609 Galileo Galilei improves Lippershey's telescope and studies the night sky and planets

1666 Isaac Newton proves that light is made up of different colors

1690 Christiaan Huygens suggests that light is made up of tiny waves

1801 Thomas Young proves Huygens' wave theory of light

1802 Humphry Davy demonstrates a continuous light using electricity

1879 Thomas Edison creates an electric light bulb with a carbon filament made from sewing thread

1901 Peter Cooper-Hewitt invents the mercury vapor, or fluorescent, lamp

1905 Albert Einstein proves that light waves are made of particles

1950s Scientists develop glass fibers in an endoscope

1960s Charles Kao suggests that fiber optic cables could be used to carry information far and fast

1960 Theodore Maiman invents the first laser

1961 James Biard and Gary Pittman invent LEDs

1976 Ed Hammer coils a narrow tube into a compact fluorescent lamp

GLOSSARY

astronomy—the study of the stars, planets, moons and other objects in space

attract—to pull something toward something else

concave—having an outline or surface that curves inward, like the inside of a bowl

convex—having an outline or surface that curves outward, like the outside of a bowl

denser—thicker or more closely packed together

electron—the smallest particle within an atom. Electrons move around the centre of an atom.

endoscope—a medical instrument that can be used to look inside the human body

evidence—the collection of information or facts that prove if something is true or not

fiber optics—the use of thin fibers of glass in bundles to send information as bursts of light

fluorescent—being able to give off light by taking in radiation

focus—the use of lenses to bend light so something can be seen more clearly

gravity—the force that pulls objects toward each other

imbalance—a lack of balance

incandescent—something that glows when it is heated to a high temperature

observe—closely monitor or study something

particle—an extremely small unit of matter

photon—a particle of light

prism—a triangular piece of glass used to produce bands of colored light

refraction—the change in direction when light moves from air into denser substances, such as water and glass

semiconductor—a material that electricity can only partly flow through

sphere—a round, ball-shaped object

theory—a scientific idea with evidence to back it up

vacuum—space containing no matter, including gasses like as air

vapor—a gas made from something that is usually a liquid or solid at normal temperatures

READ MORE

BOOKS

Bright, Michael. *Solar: From Sunshine to Light Bulb* (Source to Resource). New York City: Crabtree Publishing, 2016.

Claybourne, Anna. *Light and Sound* (Mind Webs). London, England: Wayland, 2017.

Oxlade, Chris. *The Light Bulb* (Tales of Invention). Mankato, Minn.: Heinemann, 2011.

Rompella, Natalie. *Experiments in Light and Sound with Toys and Everyday Stuff* (Fun Science). Mankato, Minn.: Capstone Press, 2015.

INTERNET SITES

Use Facthound to find Internet sites related to this book.

Visit *www.facthound.com*

Just type in 9781410987280 and go!

 Check out projects, games and lots more at **www.capstonekids.com**

ANSWERS TO QUIZ

1. The eyes; 2. Al-Hasan Ibn al-Haytham; 3. Refraction; 4. Light moves faster in air; 5. A lentil; 6. The telescope; 7. A prism; 8 Photons; 9. The electric light bulb; 10. A laser.

INDEX